THE
GARAGE SALE
HANDBOOK

Bette Krissell Harrison

**tempo
books**
GROSSET & DUNLAP
A Filmways Company
Publishers • New York

THE GARAGE SALE HANDBOOK
Copyright © 1977, 1979 by Bette Krissell Harrison

Tempo ISBN: 0-448-17198-8

To Mike, with love . . .

ACKNOWLEDGMENTS

If this book inspires you to either hold a garage sale or start a new career as a professional liquidator or flea market dealer, I can guarantee that the following people, who have generously made their time and experience available to me, have made a major contribution to that inspiration:

Clark Lang Macuch, Inc., Atlanta, Georgia
(the photographers who took the terrific photographs)

Mr. Joseph F. Picard and Ms. Louise (Lucy) Tidwell
Department of Public Safety, Forest Park, Georgia

Judy and Bruce Himelfarb
Household Liquidators of Atlanta

Reed Savage
Atlanta Flea Market

A big Thank You to Kathy O'Hehir (my editor) and to Don Orehek (the man who drew the fantastic illustrations)

Thank you: Bonnie Fisher, Bobbie Mulvey, and Doris Stahr

Thank you, Caroline

TABLE OF CONTENTS

Introduction

Think of Your Garage Sale as a Two-day
   Business.. 9

PART I
GARAGE SALES
AND OTHER HOME SALES

CHAPTER **1**
GENERAL QUESTIONS ABOUT
   GARAGE SALES...15

CHAPTER **2**
GARAGE SALES AND THE LAW...................27

CHAPTER 3

PREPARING FOR YOUR GARAGE SALE.....35
Introduction...35
Getting Out Your Merchandise............................36
Designing Your Advertising Campaign.................39
Pricing Your Merchandise....................................55
Setting Up Your Bookkeeping System.................61
The Garage Sale Command Post..........................66
The Garage Sale Cashier......................................68
Displaying Your Merchandise...............................69

CHAPTER 4

SECURITY AT YOUR GARAGE SALE............77

CHAPTER 5

SALE DAY...87

PART II
CAREERS FOR
GARAGE SALE ENTHUSIASTS

CHAPTER 6

HOW TO START A LIQUIDATION
    BUSINESS...00

CHAPTER 7

HOW TO BECOME A FLEA MARKET
    DEALER...115

INTRODUCTION

THINK OF YOUR GARAGE SALE AS A TWO-DAY BUSINESS

I want you to make a lot of money.

I want you to hold a very successful garage sale.

I want you to carefully read the following rule:

To make a lot of money and to hold a very successful garage sale, you should think of your garage sale as a two-day business!

FIRST, LET ME SHARE with you my definition of the phrase, "very successful garage sale." A very successful garage sale happens when a garage sale holder sells a lot of merchandise and makes a lot of money. After observing and holding a number of successful sales, I have concluded that there is a direct correlation between holding a very successful garage sale and thinking of the sale as a two-day business. Most people erroneously believe that if they stick up a few garage sale signs, place an ad in the newspaper, and carry their junk out to their driveway an hour before their sales begin, they have done everything they need to do to hold a garage sale. Of course, they are correct. They *have* done everything they need to do to hold a garage sale, but they *haven't* done everything they need to do to hold a very successful one.

The irony here is that these garage sale holders will probably be pleased with the results of their sales. Why shouldn't they be pleased? They will never know how much *more* merchandise they could have sold or how much *more* money they could have made had they spent more time and effort planning, organizing, and preparing for their sales.

Take Saks Fifth Avenue. Saks Fifth Avenue doesn't begin planning, organizing, and preparing for their Labor Day sale a week before Labor Day. Months of preparation go into each sale they have. Why? Because businesses want to have very successful sales; they want to *make money!*

If you are thinking, "boy, does *she* sound money-hungry," you will be on the right track. I *am* money-hungry. And, I'm not even ashamed to admit it. I *love* money. In fact, I love money so much, it prompted an ophthamologist friend to suggest that I have a pair of dollar-sign eyeglasses made to wear at my public-speaking engagements.

Whether or not someone at Saks owns a pair of dollar-sign eyeglasses remains a mystery. But it is obvious to this observer that there is someone at Saks thinking *money*, planning, organizing, and preparing Saks's sales in earnest, and dreaming of profits.

If you are serious about making money, I want you to mentally wear a pair of dollar-sign eyeglasses as you read this book. I want you to think *money* as you get out your merchandise from your closets and cupboards. I want you to say to yourself, "My garage sale is a two-day business," as you plan, organize, and prepare for your sale. And, finally, I want you to *make money* at your next garage sale. I guarantee that if you follow my instructions carefully, you will be pleased with the monetary results.

Besides being extremely profitable, a very successful garage sale is also a tremendous amount of fun. The "fun" comes from ridding your home of clutter and having the opportunity to make new acquaintances. I realize that these two activities sound rather dull when compared to the joy of *making money,* but I just thought I'd mention them.

So, good luck! And may your garage sale be even more successful than you ever imagined!

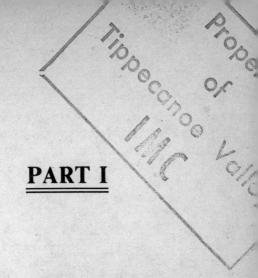

PART I

GARAGE SALES
AND
OTHER
HOME SALES

"No, George didn't get a raise . . . we had a garage sale."

• CHAPTER 1 •

GENERAL QUESTIONS ABOUT GARAGE SALES

QUESTION 1
How Can I Have a Garage Sale
When I Don't Have a Garage?

You can't—but you can hold a "porch sale" if you have a porch, or a "basement sale" if you have a basement. Most people call their sales by the name of the location they use. One exception is the "moving sale," which is usually held throughout the entire house.

If you are an apartment dweller, don't despair. You can hold a garage sale, too. Simply limit the number of people you allow into your "showroom" at any one time. If your landlord says you cannot hold a sale in your apartment, then this is the time to consider holding a sale with another person, *in*—I

Rain isn't going to prevent this patio sale from doing business.

must add—that other person's garage, basement, attic, etc.

Please note: For the purposes of this book, the term "garage sale" will be synonymous for any type of sale occurring in or around a private home—i.e., a yard sale, an attic sale, a carport sale, etc.

QUESTION 2
What Is The Best Location
For a Sale?

The *best* location for a sale meets as many of the following requirements as possible:
1. Sheltered from the weather
2. Inaccessible or can be made inaccessible to the main part of your home
3. Well-lit
4. Equipped with electrical outlets
5. Spacious
6. Exposed to passing traffic
7. Endowed with excellent parking facilities

$ WISE TIP $

If the location you have picked for your sale is not sheltered from the weather, always have an alternate location.

$ WISE TIP $

A two-day sale is a "second chance" if poor weather spoils the first day of your sale (and you simply couldn't find an alternate location).

A typical garage sale.

QUESTION 3
How Much Time Will I Need To Prepare For My Sale?

To do it right (which, of course, you want to do) allow yourself a minimum of three to four weeks to plan, prepare, and organize your sale. Remember, your garage sale is a two-day business.

QUESTION 4
When Should I Hold My Sale?

Unless you are fortunate and live in year-round warm weather, plan to hold your sale during the warmer months of the year. Weekends are the best days of the week (although many people include

Fridays when they plan a "weekend" sale). And, the best hours of the day are from 9:00 A.M. until 5:00 or 6:00 P.M. Obviously, during the summer months when the sun doesn't set until 8:30 P.M., keep your sale going until the sun sets, if you have the stamina.

QUESTION 5
How Long Should My Sale Last?

It really depends on your primary purpose for holding a sale. If you are holding a "moving sale," you most likely want to continue the sale until you sell everything. This could take a week or several weekends, depending on the amount of merchandise involved.

If, however, you are holding a sale to dispose of clutter or as a showcase for your creative talents, a weekend or even a one-day sale—i.e., a Saturday-only sale—should suffice.

QUESTION 6
Should I Hold My Sale By Myself Or With Other People?

This is a personal decision. There are advantages and disadvantages to both kinds of sales.

The advantages of holding a sale by yourself are: (1) you will have total control over all decision-making; (2) your bookkeeping system will be easier; and (3) you will not have to rely on others to do their share of the work. The disadvantages of holding a sale by yourself are: (1) you won't have other people to help with the preparations and expenses involved in the sale; (2) if you do not have a lot of merchandise to sell, your sale will not attract many potential customers; and (3) if you do not have a suitable location for a sale, you can't hold a sale at all.

If you do decide to hold a sale with other people, organize committees to handle the different aspects of the sale (checking local laws, launching an advertising campaign, picking the best location, etc.) and always appoint a chairperson to oversee the organization of the sale, settle disputes, and keep things rolling along on schedule. The chairperson should have the final say on any matter concerning the sale.

If you want to hold a street sale or a bazaar, organize your sale exactly as if you were holding a multi-individual garage sale; just add a few more committees (a committee to obtain a permit granting permission to block off a street, an entertainment committee, a refreshment committee, a security committee, etc.). It is even more important to appoint a chairperson to settle disputes and oversee the entire organization of a street sale or a bazaar because there are so many more people involved in the sale.

QUESTION 7
What Can I Sell At My Sale?

You can sell *anything* and *everything* at your sale. Even broken merchandise will sell. So don't wonder (or worry) about the "saleability" of something—just get it out, polish it up, and display it along with all your other things. Try not to smirk, guffaw, or act embarrassed or surprised when someone actually buys the item you thought you'd never sell, and for goodness sake, don't *ever* ask the person why they are buying a particular item!

Sometimes this is extremely difficult to do. You

might be so shocked to see strangers shelling out good money for what seems like junk to you that it becomes almost impossible not to ask them why they are buying what they buy. The obvious reason why you should never ask someone why they are buying something is that they might become self-conscious, rethink their motives (and sanity), and put the item back onto your display table. And you don't want *this* to happen, do you?

The only time I have ever given in to the irresistible impulse to ask someone why they were buying an item was when I sold "Daphne." I inherited Daphne from my mother and Lord knows where my mother got her! This *objet d'art,* a bawdy, overweight, fifteen-inch long, porcelain nude, reclining on a sixteen-inch plaster of paris rock, was sold (well, almost) during my second garage sale. You can't imagine how shocked I was to see a young girl cuddling Daphne and approaching my cashier's command post. I couldn't resist it. I asked her why she was buying Daphne. The young girl bubbled, "Well, my boyfriend's birthday is next week and I thought this [she held up all fifteen inches of ugliness for me to see for the last time] would make a fantastic birthday gift for him, you know, as a joke."

As I began to wrap Daphne in newspaper the girl changed her mind and placed the statue back on the display table.

Well, I hope I have made my point. Never, *ever* question the "saleability" of something. Somewhere there is someone who wants to buy absolutely anything you want to sell!

22

Who will attend my garage sale?

QUESTION 8
Should I Sell Things On Consignment At My Garage Sale?

It usually happens like this:

Your neighbor learns you are about to hold a garage sale. She doesn't want to participate, but she tells you, "I have just a few things, and would you mind terribly if I asked you to put them in your sale?" While you are deciding just how much you really *would* mind becoming a caretaker for *her* things, a good friend telephones. Your good friend says, "I have an old crib from when Johnnie was a tiny little thing. It's really pretty and I was wondering, could you, I mean, would you put it in your garage sale?" So, by now you have a neighbor on your doorstep and a friend on the telephone, and your son yells from the den. "Hey, Mom. Jeff has this brand new power saw and he wants to know if he can sell it in your garage sale. Can he, huh?"

Be smart. Say "no" to everyone. Consignment selling is a paper work jungle, and the monetary benefits to you simply aren't worth *your* trouble. Unless someone is willing to split the costs of the sale and do half the work, sweetly, but firmly, tell everyone "no."

QUESTION 9
Do I Have To Report The Money I Make At My Sale On My Income Tax Return?

Generally, no. The reasoning behind this is that whatever you sell will most likely be sold at a loss to you. The one exception is when you sell something for more than you paid for it—i.e., an antique or "collectible." If this happens, then the re-sale of these items at a higher cost is a capital gain and must be reported on your income tax return.

QUESTION 10
Who Will Attend My Sale?

Anyone looking for a bargain. And who might these people be? For starters: young couples, neighbors, friends, relatives, collectors, dealers, decorators, garage sale addicts, and total strangers.

QUESTION 11
How Much Money Can I Make At My Garage Sale?

That all depends on the kind of merchandise you are selling, the amount of merchandise, and your prices. At a two-day sale several years ago (our most expensive item was a grandmother clock), we made $950.00. The least money we have ever made was for a one-day sale ($420.00).

Find out if you live in area which requires a permit.

• CHAPTER 2 •

GARAGE SALES
AND THE LAW

IN FOREST PARK, Georgia, it all began with a few complaints. People called up the mayor and told him they didn't like the fact that Mrs. So-and-So (who lived down the street) was holding a permanent yard sale. The callers said it made their neighborhood look "junky." "Plus," they added, "on weekends we can't even park our cars in front of our homes because *her* customers park in our parking spaces. Clearly," they told the mayor, "something has got to be done."

And something *was* done. On November 18, 1974, Forest Park, Georgia, enacted Ordinance Number 74–171. Known as "The Garage Sale License Law," Ordinance 74–171 requires that a homeowner obtain a license to hold a garage sale, hold only two garage sales per year, and hold only twenty-four-hour sales. Furthermore, at the time a homeowner obtains a license to hold a garage sale, they are also handed a

FOREST PARK, GEORGIA
DEPARTMENT OF PUBLIC SAFETY

YARD SALE REGULATIONS

1. Items to be sold must be merchandise that belongs to the owner and not items that were purchased for the sale.

2. Person obtaining the permit is responsible to see that traffic on the streets or roads in the city is not impeded by shoppers.

3. There can be no signs of advertising the yard sale posted on right-of-way land or on telephone poles or any other poles, posts etc. belonging to the City or utility companies.

4. All yard sale permits are good for the day specified on the receipt only unless otherwise provided for in writing in the body of the permit.

5. Any questions which may arise that are not covered by the above may be answered by calling 366 7280 between the normal working hours of 8 am to 5 pm.

6. Permit issued must be kept at the site of the yard sale for inspection by any lawful agency of the City government.

#113 4/13/77   as

Yard sale regulations. Courtesy of The Department of Public Safety, Forest Park, Georgia.

list of additional regulations which must be adhered to in order to fully comply with Ordinance 74–171.

According to the director of public safety of Forest Park, Georgia, enforcement of Ordinance 74–171 has not been a problem. People have been complying willingly with the law, and the residential neighborhoods of Forest Park have retained their residential atmosphere.

The situation in Forest Park is not unique. Throughout the country, local governments are enacting similar legislation to regulate the number of garage sales a homeowner can hold each year and to limit the locations where garage sale signs can be posted. Some local governments have banned garage sales altogether!

Why have these local governments cracked down on garage sales? Because too many people have taken advantage of a good thing. By turning their garages, porches, basements, and yards into perpetual showrooms for selling merchandise without a business license, these greedy people have almost ruined it for everyone else who is content to clean out their closets several times a year and sell, rather than give away, what they no longer want.

To check out whether or not you live in a community that requires a license to hold a garage sale, call City Hall or your county courthouse and ask, "Do I need a license to hold a garage sale?" If you don't, fine. That's that. If you do, then you will most likely be asked to come down to City Hall or the courthouse, fill out an application form, pay a small fee ($1.00 to $3.00), and get a garage sale license.

Many people wonder if it is against the law to sell

overstuffed furniture, mattresses, food, under-garments, bathing suits, and firearms at garage sales. There are no laws on the books preventing you from selling overstuffed furniture and mattresses at your garage sale, however—and this is a gigantic "how-ever"—in order to *legally* sell them, you must adhere to the health regulations regarding their sale.

According to the Department of Agriculture of the state of Georgia, a person can sell a used mattress if that mattress has first been sterilized. Now, how does one go about sterilizing a mattress? Are you ready for this? According to the state of Georgia, there are only two acceptable ways to sterilize a mattress and they are:

METHOD #1 The Dry-Heat Method: Using this method to sterilize a mattress, you must have a suitable dry-heat chamber into which you can place the mattress, hold it at a temperature of 230° F (plus or minus 5°), and let the mattress "bake" for a minimum of one hour.

METHOD #2 The Chemical Spray Method: A suitable disinfectant effective against staphylococcus aureus, salmonella typhosa, and tubercle baccilus must be sprayed upon the mattress. The chemical disinfectant should dry rapidly and leave the mattress odor-free within one hour. The mattress must be sprayed to a depth of one-fourth-inch penetration.

Now, I bet you think this method of sterilizing mattresses is a cinch, right? Well, the clincher is: An area completely separate from any other area must be used for the spraying procedure, and this area must

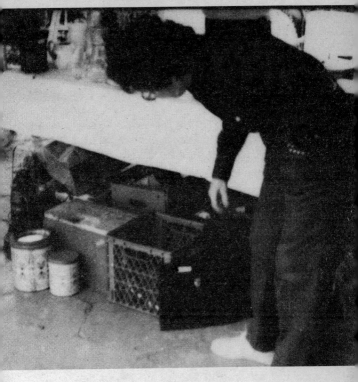

A garage sale shopper finds hidden treasures.

be used *solely* for the sterilizing of mattresses!

Just when you think you will never be able to un-load your mattress at your garage sale, Good News appears on the mattress-selling horizon. You can schlepp your mattress to a mattress-renovator, who, for a small fee, will gladly sterilize your mattress for you.

Well, I don't know about you, but I have decided that if I have any mattresses to get rid of, I am going to give them to Goodwill or the Salvation Army, whom, I am confident, will have a suitable dry-heat chamber or chemical spray chamber on their prem-ises.

If you want to sell some homemade goodies at your garage sale, take the following into consideration. The Department of Agriculture in Georgia has a twenty-seven-page pamphlet entitled *The Georgia Food Act*. If you really have a desire to adhere to the law, all I can say about selling baked goods or pre-serves at your garage sale is check with your local office of the Department of Agriculture.

Regarding undergarments and bathing suits, it is hard to believe, but I have called every state, county, and federal agency I could think of, and no one I have spoken to can recall a law prohibiting their sale at garage sales.

The only requirements the federal government has concerning the sale of firearms at garage sales are:

1. That the firearm is from your own private collec-tion—i.e., you are not a dealer in firearms.
2. That the seller ask the buyer the following ques-tions before writing up a bill of sale:

    a. Are you over eighteen years of age? (if the weapon is a rifle)

    b. Are you over twenty-one years of age? (if the weapon is a handgun)

    c. Are you a resident of this state?

    d. Are you a convicted felon or a fugitive from justice?

3. That the seller write up a bill of sale with the date of the sale and the buyer's name, address, and driver's license number written on it.

All this red tape is for the seller's protection. If the weapon is used in a crime, the seller will be able to show the bill of sale to the authorities and prove that he did not have possession of the firearm at the time the crime was committed.

Whether or not you want to sell overstuffed furniture, mattresses, food, undergarments, bathing suits, and firearms at your garage sale is a decision that should be based upon the laws regarding those types of sales.

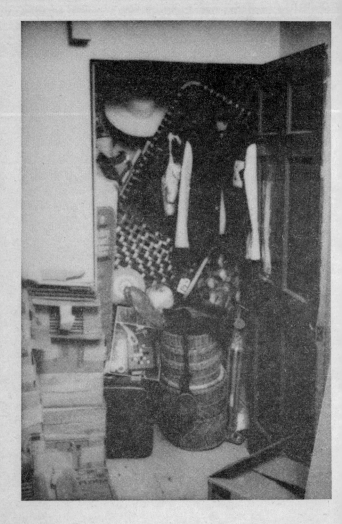

A bulging junk closet.

CHAPTER 3

PREPARING FOR YOUR GARAGE SALE

Introduction

YOU SHOULD BEGIN several of the activities discussed in this chapter almost immediately after you have decided to hold a garage sale. For instance, it is never too early to begin getting out and cleaning up your merchandise or designing your advertising campaign.

Pricing and tagging merchandise and setting up your bookkeeping system can wait until the week before your sale. Displaying your merchandise and setting up your "command post" can wait until the day before sale day, but details such as cleaning, repairing, and putting up signs are time consuming and *should be done well in advance of sale day*.

The best tip is that the morning of sale day should be strictly for making *very last minute* changes in prices and display.

Getting Out Your Merchandise

You will be absolutely amazed at how much you will enjoy opening up your closets and pulling out merchandise to sell at your sale. There is a great deal of pleasure derived from the anticipation of selling things you don't like or—all right, I'll say it—even *hate*.

So, go to your cupboards, your junk closets, and your pantries. Open up those drawers, those boxes, those cartons and *have fun!* Put on those dollar-sign eyeglasses. If you haven't used something in two years, you probably will never use it. If you've never liked something, chances are you will never miss it. For encouragement, please let me share with you a wonderful truism: I have never missed anything I sold at one of my garage sales. *Never!*

Now, if that isn't inspiring, I don't know what is!

Here is a list of suggested items you can sell at your garage sale:

Antiques	*Glassware*
Appliances	*Knick-knacks*
Artificial and dried flowers	*Magazines*
	Mirrors
Automobile accessories	*Nostalgia items, of any kind*
Bicycles	
Books	*Office equipment*
Cameras	*Paintings*
Candles	*Pianos*
China	*Plants, plastic and real*
Clocks	*Pots and pans*
Clothing, especially children's clothing and	*Records, especially jazz and early rock*
	Sports equipment

"Your sign says you buy anything!"

outerwear garments	*Tablecloths*
Collectibles	*Tools*
Crafts	*Toys*
Crystal	*Typewriters*
Electrical tools	*Shells, rocks*
Furniture	*Suitcases*
Games	

$ WISE TIP $

Before you begin selecting merchandise to sell at your garage sale, pick an area in your home to store the merchandise until sale day.

$ WISE TIP $

Polish, clean, and repair (within reason) everything you want to sell. Even an old washing machine will sell for more money if it is sparkling clean.

$ WISE TIP $

Wash, iron, or dry-clean any clothes you wish to sell. Also, size the clothes. Pin shoes and gloves together with their mates.

$ WISE TIP $

If possible, have plenty of inexpensive items for children. This serves two purposes: (1) many people will bring children to your sale, and if you have things that interest children, the children's enthusiasm may rub off on their parents; and (2) if you have a

Shoes should be paired, sized and lined up side-by-side. Don't throw them in a box like this garage sale holder did.

"children's corner," the children will amuse themselves, leaving their parents free to do some serious shopping.

Designing Your Advertising Campaign

Many times, garage sale holders are disappointed by the number of people who attend their sales. Putting ads in newspapers and hanging signs on telephone poles is not enough. Believe it or not, there is a right way and a wrong way—or better put—an effective way and an ineffective way to word a garage sale sign or classified ad.

An effective advertising campaign for any product

"Nora, did you advertise Star Wars *or the fact that we are holding a garage sale?"*

should always: (1) **identify** the product or service clearly and simply; and (2) **entice** the reader to act on the information provided.

There are three techniques used in an effective advertising campaign. They are: (1) word of mouth; (2) garage sale signs; and (3) newspaper classified ads.

Word of Mouth

This is absolutely one of the best ways to advertise a garage sale. However, you must know how to make it work. Obviously, you tell everyone you know about your garage sale and ask them to tell everyone they know about your sale, but don't make your garage sale sound ordinary when you tell them about it. Don't say:

> *"Oh, Nancy, by the way, on May 17th and 18th, some of us are going to have a garage sale at my home. Hope you can make it. Oh yes, please tell everyone you know about it . . . huh."*

> **Instead, say:**
> *"Wow, Nancy! On May 17th and 18th, a bunch of us are going to have a super garage sale at my house. We're selling lots of really fantastic stuff: crystal, antiques, tools, children's toys, knick-knacks, and even an antique brass bed. It's going to be the greatest sale this neighborhood has ever had! You really shouldn't miss it! Please tell everyone you know about it!"*

Now, *that's* salesmanship! In addition to enticing Nancy to attend your sale, your enthusiasm might

41

even rub off on her when she tells *her* friends. You'll find that one minute spent talking about your sale with a friend means many more customers will be shopping at your garage sale.

In addition, tell grocery clerks, carpool drivers, your children's teachers, your postman . . .

Tell everyone!

$ WISE TIP $

Some communities have local radio stations that will be happy to announce your garage sale. Why don't you check out this avenue for free advertising?

$ WISE TIP $

Enthusiasm is contagious!

$ WISE TIP $

Does your church or club have a newsletter or bulletin? Why not see if you can get a notice of your garage sale published a week or so before your sale day?

Garage Sale Signs

The five biggest mistakes people make concerning their garage sale signs are:

1. They make their signs too big
2. They put too much information on their signs
3. They don't have enough signs
4. They put up their signs too late, and
5. They make their signs themselves.

A paper plate makes an eye-catching, staked garage sale sign.

MISTAKE #1 They Make Their Signs Too Big: Have you ever driven past a garage sale sign with its corners folded over so that the only legible thing on the sign was the cryptic message, "arage Sa." If all you could read was "arage Sa," the garage sale sign was too big.

Where is it written that garage sale signs need to be big? Bigger isn't better in this case. In fact, bigger is worse and there is a very good reason why bigger is worse. Signs that are bigger than 8½" by 14" cannot wrap snugly around a telephone pole, so they flap in the wind and fold over. Consequently, the message is not easily visible.

Big garage sale signs are not only unnecessary, they are impractical. I have seen large wooden garage sale signs lying on the ground and tremendous tin and aluminum signs bent beyond recognition. Believe me, nothing—absolutely nothing—withstands the abuse of weather better than a paper 8½" by 14" sign snugly wrapped around a telephone pole.

Even if you live in a community that has (and enforces) a law prohibiting the use of telephone poles as handy advertising props (thus forcing homeowners to stake their garage sale signs), you still do not need to have large garage sale signs. One of the most effective garage sale signs I have ever seen was a small paper plate attached to a wooden stake. Or, you can simply take two 8½" by 14" signs, place them back to back, put a wooden stake between them, and presto! You have a super garage sale sign!

The *only* exception I can think of to the 8½" by 14" rule would be the garage sale sign placed at the entrance of your driveway. Make that one big. The

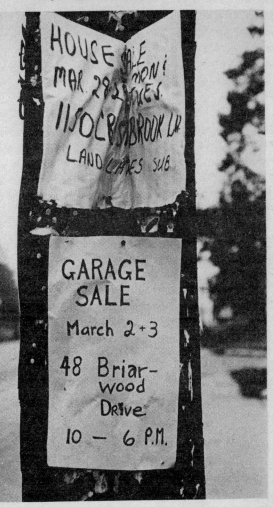

Use 8½" x 11" or 8½" x 14" paper for your signs if you want them to wrap snugly around telephone poles.

reasoning behind this exception to the rule is (1) you want to attract as many passersby as you possibly can, and (2) you don't put a driveway garage sale sign out until the morning of your sale, so the sign never has time to succumb to weather.

MISTAKE #2 They Put Too Much Information on Their Signs: Have you ever seen a garage sale sign with so much information written on it that all you could read was "Garage Sale," and the rest of the sign was a big blur? The only information a garage sale sign should contain is:

1. The kind of sale it is—moving sale, garage sale, yard sale, etc.
2. The date(s) of the sale—Not the days of the week, but the *date(s)* of the sale. Saturday? Which Saturday? This Saturday? Next Saturday?
   Preferable: November 10, 1979
3. The time of the sale
4. The address of the sale
5. The words, "Cash Only," if applicable, and
6. Directional arrows pointing *to* the sale.

Don't add a list of your merchandise to your garage sale signs. Don't put cute little sayings on your signs. Don't draw clever designs. The only thing added information does is clutter up your garage sale sign and turn it into a big blur.

MISTAKE #3 They Don't Have Enough Signs: Flood your neighborhood with garage sale signs. Make it seem like your sale will be the greatest one your community will ever have.

Breaking all the rules by using cute sayings, clever drawings, and larger than 8½" x 14", this Hand-me-down Heyday sign is still effective. But who wants to spend their time making up more than a few of these?

MISTAKE #4 They Put Up Their Signs Too Late: Try to put your signs up at least one week prior to sale day; this gives your potential customers a chance to plan to attend your sale. Unfortunately, some garage sale holders put their signs up so near the day of their sale that many people who would have attended can't, because they have made other plans for the day.

MISTAKE #5 They Make Their Signs Themselves: If you knew how inexpensive it is to have a professional printer make your signs, you would probably never again make another garage sale sign yourself. It is definitely worth your time and money to check into the cost of having a printer make your signs because:

1. Printers use waterproof ink,
2. Printers can print signs a great deal faster than you can make them, and
3. Merely by selling a few items at your sale, you will recoup the cost of having your signs professionally printed.

The last time I had a garage sale, I had thirty signs printed and it cost $6.00. Consider having a professional printer make your signs for you. You will be pleased with the results.

HOW TO HAVE YOUR GARAGE SALE SIGNS PROFESSIONALLY PRINTED

Take a piece of 8 ½" by 14" white paper (legal size) and write the essential information about your sale on it. Take the original to a "quick copy" printer. Ask him to use the sturdiest paper he has and photocopy whatever number of signs you want. I have found that the best color combination for garage sale signs (by "best," I mean you can see the sign from far away) is bright yellow paper with black ink. In many cases, the printer will actually print your signs for you while you wait.

I ask you. What could be easier?

If you do decide to make your own signs, use waterproof ink and print legibly only the essential information. The best size paper to use is 8 ½″ x 14″.

$ WISE TIP $

If you live in a community that doesn't allow garage sales signs *at all*, here is a nifty idea I picked up during one of my public speaking engagements:

> *Attach two big garage sale signs back to back with elastic tape. Pay children to wear these garage sale "posters" while they ride their bicycles around your neighborhood. Apparently, this tactic works out well for the children (who earn their spending money), parents (who get to advertise their garage sales), and City Council (no garage sale signs are stuck in the ground or tacked onto telephone poles).*

$ WISE TIP $

Don't forget to put garage sale signs on grocery store, church, and organization bulletin boards.

$ WISE TIP $

Put signs at every intersection near your home and in every direction people will be passing.

$ WISE TIP $

If it is all right to put garage sale signs on telephone poles in your community, please ask permission of property owners *before* you put up any signs on "their" telephone poles. And, *always remove all your signs after your sale is over!*

Newspaper Classified Ads

The philosophy behind advertising your garage sale in a newspaper radically differs from the one behind garage sale signs. On your signs, you want to say as little as possible so that your sign is legible to a driver of an automobile passing at 30 or 40 mph. In your newspaper ad, however, you want to say as much as possible so the reader of the ad can't pass up the golden opportunity to attend your sale.

You must always keep in mind that you are competing with all the other people who are advertising *their* garage sales in the newspaper. Every weekend edition of the newspaper contains dozens of garage sale ads, and garage sale goers couldn't possibly attend each one of them. This is why you want to make your ad *stand out* from all the others. Two excellent ways to make your ad *stand out* are (1) by using capital letters on the first line of print, and (2) by naming

"You're right, dear, it is a garage sale sign."

particular items you plan to sell. For example, this ad sounds very uninteresting:

> *Garage Sale: Loads of things. Sat. and Sun. 10:00* A.M. *on 1420 Candy Drive.*

And this ad sounds *very* interesting:

> *FABULOUS GARAGE SALE THIS SAT. AND SUN.: Antique brass bed, grandfather clock, green velvet sofa, crystal, Stratfordshire china, children's clothes and toys, bric-a-brac, Black and Decker power tools, Panasonic T.V., old records—1420 Candy Drive. 10:00* A.M. *on.*

Which sale would *you attend?*

Whether or not to include your telephone number in your ad is always a big question. There is one major *pro* for including it and one major *con* against including it. The question you will have to answer is: Does the big *pro* outweigh the big *con?*

Big Pro: *You can give directions to your home.*

Big Con: *Your phone will ring off the hook for the duration of your sale. This wouldn't be so bad if the only information people wanted was directions to your home. But, unfortunately, a great number of these callers want to know if you have a particular item for sale. If you do, great. They will come to your sale. If you don't, they won't come to your sale. By speaking to them over*

> Consignments accepted. Antiques, bric-a-brac, clothes, etc.
>
> # GARAGE SALE
>
> Rugs, misc. furn., etc. 460 W. Paces Ferry Rd. 10 a.- 4 p. Sat.
>
> GARAGE Sale. Saturday 25, 10—4, Furniture, bunk mattresses, clothing and bric-a-brac. 3636 Inman Dr. N.E., behind Oglethorpe University, off Woodrow Way.
>
> GARAGE Sale, various and sundry items from "A" to "Z". Saturday only, 9:30 A.M. until 6

Garage sale classified ads.

the telephone, you ruin your chances of their attending your sale to look for these items, perhaps not finding them, but still buying other items that may catch their eyes.

$ WISE TIP $

Always give the name of the manufacturer, antique "period," or craftsmen of the items you are selling. A little snobbery never hurts. If you have a Steinway piano for sale, say so. Waterford crystal? Say so.

$ WISE TIP $

If you live in an out-of-the-way section of town, spend a bit more money for your ad and include excellent directions to your home.

$ WISE TIP $

Never mention an article for sale you don't really have just because you think doing so will attract more customers for your other merchandise.

$ WISE TIP $

Why not use holidays in your ad? For example:

GREAT CHRISTMAS BARGAINS IN OCTOBER at our fabulous garage sale or WE'RE HAVING OUR OWN BIG LABOR DAY SALE this Saturday at our super garage sale.

WHEN TO PLACE YOUR AD

Remember, newspapers have deadlines for placing classified advertising. Some newspapers need as much as one week's notice *before* publication. Check your local newspaper's deadline for placing classified ads as soon as you decide to hold a garage sale. You don't have to place the ad at that time, but at least you will know when the deadline is. The best time to advertise your sale is a week in advance.

What Is Market Research?

Market research is a combination of three activities which, when combined, give you an excellent idea of how to price your merchandise. Here are some suggestions for doing market research:

1. Check Store Catalogs: A Sears or J. C. Penney catalog are invaluable resources for learning what items cost. You must know the price of a new television set before you can put a price on a seven-year-old model.

2. Check Prices At Other Garage Sales: It is a smart idea to attend other garage sales and see how other people price seven-year-old television sets, fifteen-year-old washing machines, or whatever. After going to several garage sales, you will begin to learn the present market value of a variety of different items.

3. Have A Professional Appraise Valuable Items: Always obtain a professional appraisal for antiques, collectibles, jewelry, and other valuables you may want to sell. You will never get the full appraised value of something you sell at your garage sale, but at least you will know what the item is worth and what a "reasonable" price would be for it.

Pricing Your Merchandise

The reason many people have so much difficulty pricing their merchandise is that they truly don't understand the nature of a garage sale. A garage sale is not a retail store, a discount house, or an antique shop. *A garage sale is a garage sale!* The following three concepts should greatly aid in teaching you the basic nature of a garage sale. Read these concepts *very carefully* and as many times as you must in order to fully appreciate and understand the garage sale philosophy. Once you have them ingrained in your heart, mind, and soul, pricing merchandise will be easy:

THE GOLDEN AXIOM OF GARAGE SALE PRICING

Every person who attends your sale is looking for a bargain.

THE GOLDEN RULE OF GARAGE SALE PRICING

An item is a "bargain" when it is priced according to:

(1) its original cost,
(2) its physical condition,
(3) its present market value, and
(4) how much the garage sale holder wants to get rid of it!

THE GOLDEN SUCCESS STORY OF GARAGE SALE PRICING

The bargain hunters found the bargains and the garage sale holder made a small fortune.

It doesn't matter if you are selling "period" antiques, magnificent handmade quilts, or a lawnmower purchased as recently as last spring. If you want to sell a lot of merchandise, you need to price your merchandise not according to how much it is worth, but how much you want to get rid of it. How much something is worth, of course, is important, because it will determine the basic price for an item.

But, still, when it comes to garage sales, the bottom line is: People go to garage sales because they are looking for bargains, and if you don't have bargains at your sale, people are not going to buy your merchandise.

You see, making money at your garage sale boils down to quantity, not quality. One dollar items add up. You can not rely on the "big sale." You must rely on selling many things at bargain prices.

Now, this doesn't mean that you have to give the stuff away. If you do your market research before your sale and get professional appraisals for valuables like antiques, collectibles, and jewelry, you are still going to make a bundle even though your merchandise is priced reasonably.

How To Find A Price For An Item

In football, a good quarterback is said to have "the touch," which means he has an uncanny ability to throw a football exactly where that football should be thrown (to the right place *and* at the right time) for a receiver to catch it. Basically, pricing merchandise is similar. You should try to develop "the touch" for pricing your merchandise. You must learn how low you can go without giving something away, and still price an item high enough to make the most money you can.

Over the years I have developed two methods of pricing merchandise that work quite well for me. Most of the time I use both methods for *each* piece of merchandise at my sale. I know this sounds laborious, but it isn't. It takes a fraction of a second to come up with a price for an item, because after a while you let "the touch" take over for you and pricing merchandise becomes easy to do.

METHOD #1 Put Yourself In The Potential Buyer's Shoes: Pretend you are a potential buyer for each item. Keeping all your market research in the back of your mind, ask yourself what *you* would pay for the item. Remember, since you are the buyer, you want a bargain!

METHOD #2 The Descending Order of Prices: Using this method, you mentally place each item into a price category reflecting the item's physical condition. An item that meets the criteria for Category #1 should have a higher price than the same item meeting the criteria for Category #2.

Don't be shocked, but a good starting price for any item falling into Category #1 would be somewhere a little over or a little under half the price of the item's original cost.

Note: You should not use this method for antiques and collectibles.

Category #1
Item is new, still in original box, and is the most recent model or version of item.

Category #2
Item is slightly used but still looks quite new and may even have original box.

Category #3
Item is obviously used but still in excellent condition.

"Just for a second, I had the most horrible thought. I was wondering how much we could get for Roger at our garage sale next week."

Category #4

Item is new but dented or chipped, with missing parts or pieces of sets. Item can be repaired or missing pieces replaced.

Category #5

Item is very used, in terrible shape, but can be repaired.

Category #6

Item isn't new and it isn't old enough to be an antique. In any case, it is broken beyond repair. *No! Do not throw out!* Put a very low price on item. Believe it or not, someone may still buy it.

How To Find A Price For An
Antique or Collectible

Look at the appraised value of the item. Think "bargain" and stand in the buyer's shoes. A price will pop into your mind. Now, drop a few dollars off *that* price.

$ WISE TIP $

As you price items, think about your bottom line price for them. Then, add a few cents (if the item is inexpensive) or a few dollars (if expensive). Doing this will leave you room for bargaining. Never add so much to the price that the item ceases to be a bargain.

$ WISE TIP $

Truthfully, you can *never* put too low a price on an item, only too high a price.

$ WISE TIP $

Halfway through your sale, lower the prices on the items that haven't sold.

Setting Up Your Bookkeeping System

The purpose of having a bookkeeping system for your garage sale is to make the handling of money, both during and after the sale, as fair and as easy as possible. Garage sale bookkeeping is simple to learn and will never become a problem if *everyone connected with the sale* understands the method(s) to be used and completes preparations for the bookkeeping system *before the sale begins.*

The three bookkeeping methods described in this book all necessitate your using self-sticking, removable labels as price tags. Just like letting a professional printer make your signs for you, this is a case in which spending a little bit more money (a package of self-sticking, removable labels costs about $3.00) saves you priceless time, and makes not only bookkeeping easier, but changing prices of items during your sale easier, too. Please, do yourself another favor and forget making price tags out of masking tape, writing prices on tiny scraps of paper and then taping them to your merchandise, or using price tags with string. Self-sticking, removable labels are easy to apply, easy to remove, and will never mar the surface of your merchandise.

The bookkeeping methods discussed in this book will all work; however, there are advantages and disadvantages to each one of them. For example, Method #1—The Tag And Forget Method—is the easiest and least time-consuming but can't be used for a multi-individual sale, and for those individuals who want a record of what transpired during their sales, this method is quite useless. Whereas, Method #3— The Tag And Know Method—is time-consuming to set up but gives you a complete record of the items sold and their prices. Since you are continually marking down the prices of items depending on whether or not they are selling, this tagging method offers a complete record of price changes.

You are going to have to choose between what is easy and vague, and what is time-consuming but gives the most information when the sale is over.

METHOD #1 The Tag and Forget Method: The seller writes the price of each item on a self-sticking, removable label and attaches the price tag to the item. When the item is sold, the seller removes the price tag and throws it in the trash can. (I told you this was easy and vague.)

Note: *Do not use this method if you are holding a multi-individual sale unless each seller acts as their own cashier!*

The "Tag and Forget" method.

METHOD #2 The Tag And Wonder Method: Each seller puts a price tag on each item being sold. Each tag notates the price of the item and the seller's code, which is usually one of the seller's initials. When an item is sold, the cashier removes the price tag from the item and places the tag on the "sellers' master list." At the end of the sale, the cashier adds up all the price tags in each column of the list and divides the proceeds of the sale according to the sums at the bottom of each seller's column.

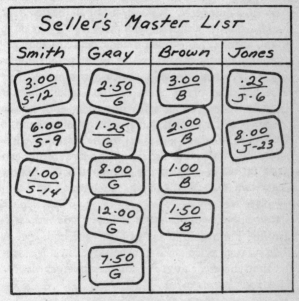

The "Tag and Wonder" method.

$ WISE TIP $

If you want to make this method even easier, buy different-colored, self-sticking, removable labels. Each individual uses a different color price tag.

$ WISE TIP $

If you are holding a sale by yourself and want to use this method, simply take a piece of paper, stick your price tags on it as you sell things, and forget using a code.

METHOD #3 The Tag And Know Method: Each seller prepares a numbered inventory list of all the items for sale. Each seller writes on each price tag: (1) the price of the item; (2) the seller's code; and (3) the corresponding number of that item on the seller's inventory list. As items are sold, the cashier removes their price tags and places them on the "sellers' master list." At the end of the sale, the cashier adds up the price tags of each seller, and gives each seller the total of all money earned and a list of the price tag numbers sold. Then, the seller, when convenient, can check off the items from the numbered list and know exactly what was sold and what each item's final selling price was.

Remember, you can use different-colored, self-sticking, removable labels with this method, too. A code on each price tag is unnecessary, but it is essential that you *don't forget to add the inventory number from your inventory list!*

$ WISE TIP $

If you are holding a sale by yourself and wish to use this method, follow the above instructions but forget using a code on your price tags. Simply remove the price tags from the items as they are sold and

Smith's List

No.	Item	Price	Sold
1.	Bicycle	20.00	
2.	Glass Car	2.00	
3.	Tiffany Lamp	100.00	
4.	Raincoat	4.00	
5.	Painting	15.00	
6.	Copper Pot	8.00	
7.	Typewriter	12.00	
8.	Suitcase	3.00	
9.	Bamboo Chair	6.00	
10.	Mirror	1.50	
11.	Perfume tray	6.00	
12	Old Book	3.00	
13.	Dried flowers	2.00	
14.	Book-ends	1.00	

The "Tag and Know" method.

place their price tags next to the corresponding number on your inventory list.

$ WISE TIP $

Not every seller needs to use the same method of bookkeeping; some may want to know what they sold and how much each item sold for and others may not. As long as each seller uses a code or a different color price tag, mixing bookkeeping methods #2 and #3 is fine.

The Garage Sale Command Post

It is extremely important for you to have a central location or "command post" for your garage sale. This is where your cashier should sit, where extra price tags should be kept, and where valuable items such as jewelry, small collectibles, coins, etc., should be displayed. You should try to locate your command post in an area able to accommodate a small crowd of people comfortably, because the cashier can only take care of one person at a time. It is also wise to locate your command post near the exit (for security reasons).

You should keep the following equipment and supplies at your command post:

Extra self-sticking, removable labels

Extra pens

Plenty of newspaper, cartons, and shopping bags for wrapping items

Extension cords

"Debbie, take over for Bruce in kitchen utensils . . . Marie, relieve your mother in home furnishings."

A scratch pad

A legal pad (the seller's master list)

A cashbox with approximately $100.00 in small bills and change

A radio (optional)

A small adding machine or electronic calculator

A coffee machine (optional)

Appraisals of valuable merchandise

A receipt book for cash sales

The Garage Sale Cashier

It's a good idea to have only one person be your garage sale cashier for the duration of your sale. There should be, however, someone else familiar with the duties of the cashier so that the cashier can take breaks when needed.

Basically, the duties of the cashier are simple: *Collect and keep a record of the money received during the sale.* Thus, the person who acts as cashier should have a good head for figures, be able to work well and quickly under pressure, and prefer a sedentary job, such as the handling of money, rather than a more active job, such as selling merchandise or acting as a security guard.

Since there will be periods that are quite hectic during your sale, the cashier should have a helper. The cashier's helper should remove price tags as items are sold, wrap items in newspaper, and tell the cashier of

Use big items to display smaller ones. A watch and a cameo ribbon-necklace draped on top of a ceramic ashtray makes a pretty display.

any price changes that would necessitate new price tags being made.

The cashier and the helper should sit at the "command post" of your sale.

Displaying Your Merchandise

People have two different philosophies concerning how a garage sale should "look." One group believes a garage sale should look as junky as possible. I believe those who follow this philosophy reason that if a place looks messy, it will lead the customer to think that the garage sale holder is completely inex-

This sale looks so pretty that I can't tell if it is a garage sale

or a boutique.

perienced and might well be literally giving things away. Some sellers also believe that having the place look a mess will evoke something of the fun of an old attic.

Well, I am of the opposing philosophy. I believe your garage sale should have the atmosphere of a fashionable boutique rather than that of a junk shop. I feel you should display your merchandise as attractively as possible, because, as I said earlier, even an old washing machine will sell for more money if it is cleaned up and displayed nicely.

And so, keeping this in mind, here are some suggestions for turning your garage into a "showroom":

1. Put some sort of covering on each display table. Use old sheets or old tablecloths.

2. Use merchandise to display other merchandise. For example, a perfume tray can be used to display costume jewelry or evening bags.

3. If you have lamps to sell, leave them lit, even in the daytime. If you are not selling any lamps, bring sturdy ones from your home to the sale area. Put big "Not For Sale" signs on the lamps you bring from home. I realize that this seems like a lot more work, but the results will be worth it. Dark garages are, let's face it, dark garages and not very conducive to putting people in a happy, *buying,* frame of mind.

4. Always display smaller items in front of larger ones.

5. Hang all pictures or paintings, or lean them against a wall.

6. Always hang clothes on a clothesline or a clothes rack rather than piling them on a table.

7. Books should be stacked so their titles can be easily seen. Do not throw them in a box.

8. Store record albums in a carton so people can flip through them easily. But *don't* place the carton in the sun—records have been known to melt!

9. If at all possible, why not check out the possibility of designing a temporary dressing room so customers can try on clothing?

10. Try to have a long, vertical mirror handy so customers can see themselves as they try on clothing.

11. If you are selling a broken item, it is a good idea to take an index card and write the following information: Either (1) exactly what is broken and some suggestions on how to fix it, or (2) if the item is irreparable, then some ideas on what you can turn the item into with a little loving care—i.e., an old coffee grinder could be made into a planter.

12. Always provide wide aisles between your display tables so customers can have plenty of room to move around—otherwise accidents could happen.

13. Leave a radio playing during your sale. The radio should be played softly enough so that the effect is that of background music rather than a live band.

$ WISE TIP $

Many times you can borrow a clothes rack from an organization or from a local department store.

$ WISE TIP $

Put a big sign up where *everyone* can see it. The sign should read, "If you break it, *you* take it!"

$ WISE TIP $

Just a reminder—never wait until sale day to begin setting up your display tables. Even if you have to work until midnight on the eve of sale day, get your display tables up and your merchandise priced, tagged, and attractively displayed *before sale day!*

"I changed my mind again, Harry. I think the love seat will go well with the pots and pans."

How to handle shoplifters.

• CHAPTER 4 •

SECURITY AT YOUR GARAGE SALE

AN EXCELLENT SECURITY SYSTEM will discourage a shoplifter from shopping for the ultimate bargain—a freebie—at your garage sale or stop a thief from stealing the most valuable item—your cashbox. I have stopped trying to figure out why we haven't had any crimes at our garage sales—is it because only honest people attend them, or because our security system is so good? Now, whenever we hold a sale, I just set up the system that has worked in the past and cross my fingers.

The security system I use is actually a list of rules to which I fervently adhere each time I hold a garage sale. I can't promise you that if you follow these rules you will never have a theft at your sale. But, I can promise you that if you follow these rules carefully, the possibility of theft will be greatly reduced.

Never Leave Your Garage Sale Unattended

If a customer wants to see merchandise that is at a different location from your sale area, make sure that someone you know minds your showroom for you. Most customers will understand this precaution and will be happy to wait until you can find someone to sit in for you at your sale.

$ WISE TIP $

Unless you know the person, never ask one of your customers to sit in for you at your sale.

Never Let Anyone Into Your Home

There are only three reasons why a customer will want to enter your home:

1. To see a piece of furniture
2. To use your telephone
3. To use your bathroom

If people want to enter your home for Reason #1 (garage sale business), fine. But escort them to the merchandise and then back to the sale area. Don't "presume" anything about them ("she's a sweet, little ol' lady who couldn't hurt a fly," etc.).

If a customer wants to enter your home for Reasons #2 and #3, say "no." Now, because it is extremely difficult to say no to grandmother types, mothers with small children, and other pleasant-looking people, I want you to practice saying no out loud until it becomes second nature to you. You must understand that during the hectic pace of sale day, your reasoning and common sense will be strained. Therefore, you must be programmed to say no to all these innocent-looking people, because they may use these excuses to get into your home and case it for some other, not-so-innocent-looking people.

Never let anyone into your home for any reason other than garage sale business. And never allow them in your home unless they are escorted by you or someone helping at your sale.

If you think I want you to be paranoid about letting people into your home, you are right. I *do* want you to be paranoid. I also want you to be able to say after your sale is over, "Gee, I can't figure out if only honest people attended our sale or if our security system was excellent. All I know is, we didn't have any problems with crime at our garage sale."

$ WISE TIP $

Why not check out where the nearest public telephone and bathroom are? Then, if someone asks to use your telephone, you can smile your nicest smile and say, "I'm sorry but our policy is to not let anyone inside our home. But there's a public telephone two blocks away at the corner drugstore."

Keep Items of Exceptional Value At Your Command Post

Jewelry, coins, stamps, and other small items of exceptional value should be kept under close surveillance. The best location for these items is your command post.

Have As Many People As Possible Watching The Sale Area

Nothing else will intimidate most potential shoplifters and thieves like people watching over the sale area. Your "watchers" shouldn't give the appearance of prison guards, but they should be pleasantly alert —if there is such a thing.

$ WISE TIP $

Older children make excellent watchers and seem to truly enjoy the responsibility of helping you.

$ WISE TIP $

If you see an individual lingering in any one spot for a long time, go over and ask, "May I help you?" or say, "Let me tell you about this clock." If the person *is* a potential shoplifter, he or she will soon become discouraged by your constant intrustions, and if a potential customer, he or she will probably be grateful for your help.

Keep the Doors and Windows To Your Home Locked

This rule applies to before, during and after your garage sale. It can't hurt to be cautious.

$ WISE TIP $

If you live in a "high-crime" area, *don't hold a garage sale!* Find a friend who lives in a safer neighborhood and hold a multi-individual sale there.

"I call it garage sale chic."

Never Approach A Shoplifter Who Is In The Middle Of Shoplifting

If you actually see someone shoplifting, never approach them. Decide if the item is of such value that you want to notify the police. Most of the time, it won't be. But if it is, never hesitate to call the police.

If something is stolen at your sale, including cash, you can report whatever is stolen as a loss on your income tax return. So, if you see a shoplifting crime in progress, you are going to have to make a quick decision. Do you want to draw attention to the incident (and unsettle the rest of your customers with the appearance of a patrol car), or do you want to let it go and report the theft as a loss on your income tax return?

Do You Want A "Cash Only" Policy At Your Garage Sale?

Many people believe that a "cash only" policy is the best way to handle the payment for merchandise at a garage sale. We have never had a cash only policy, and we have never had a single check bounce. So, it's up to you whether or not to enforce this policy at your sale.

The advantages of having a cash only policy are: (1) you will never have any bounced checks, and (2) the handling of cash is somewhat easier than having to endorse and deposit a bunch of checks. The disadvantages are: (1) many people don't like to carry large amounts of cash, and (2) passers-by, who didn't know about your garage sale (or cash only policy), may stop in, see something they want to buy, and not be able to buy it because they don't have enough money with them. Remember: A great many of your customers will be impulse buyers, and if they have to schlepp back to their homes to get more money or run to the drugstore to cash a check, they may say to themselves, "It isn't worth it," and leave.

$ WISE TIP $

If you want a cash only policy at your garage sale, then you must say so in your classified ad and on all your signs.

$ WISE TIP $

If you don't want a cash only policy at your garage sale, you will be wise to follow these instructions for accepting customers' personal checks:

When a customer hands you a check, ask to see a driver's license and two other pieces of identification with addresses on them. Look and see if all the addresses match. If two match and one doesn't, ask the customer why. Most people will answer that they have recently moved. Accept this answer. But, if a customer has *more than two* different addresses on their identification, tell them that it is your policy to ask for payment in cash under these circumstances.

$ WISE TIP $

A high check number in the upper right-hand corner of a pesonal check (e.g., no. 5611) is an excellent sign. It means that the person has been dealing with one particular bank for a long time.

Obviously, the purpose for all the precautions described in this chapter is to decrease the opportunity for theft at your garage sale. You will never know if people really are basically honest or if your security system made them honest. But who cares, as long as the result is a happy one?

What to look for when you accept a check.

This garage sale holder made her garage sale look like an outdoor boutique.

• CHAPTER 5 •

SALE DAY

WHAT CAN YOU EXPECT on sale day? Well, you can expect it to be filled with people, excitement, and surprises.

Sale Day Will Be Filled With People

On or before sale day, you are going to discover that friends, relatives, neighbors, and total strangers have suddenly become "the public." Keeping in mind that you are opening your door to the public and, that the public is a mixed bag of individuals, here, then, is a primer on how to handle the various types of people who will attend your sale.

1. The Pleasant, Friendly Customer: Most of the people who will attend your sale will be exceptionally pleasant, friendly, and as excited and happy to buy something from you as you are to sell something to them. Every time you sell an item to a pleasant, friendly customer, give them a big smile and a sincere Thank You!

2. The Indifferent Customer: I don't know how else to describe this type of customer except to say that they will be indifferent, will attend your sale either alone or with a friend, will swiftly case the display tables and then, just as quickly, disappear. The best way to treat indifferent customers is to: (1) understand that they are in a hurry and simply don't want to waste time at a sale where nothing interests them, and (2) try not to get your feelings hurt because they have unofficially proclaimed your junk to be ... well, to be junk!

3. Nervy Nancys: I can almost guarantee that you will have your fair share of Nervy Nancys arriving on your doorstep or telephoning you (they probably get your phone number from the city directory) even before your sale officially begins. Nervy Nancys can be dealers (who want the pick of your merchandise), collectors (who want the pick of your collectibles), or just plain nervy strangers who want to attend your sale before it officially begins.

Should you let Nervy Nancy dealers, collectors, and strangers attend your sale before everyone else? We don't think so, and we tell them we don't feel it would be fair to our other customers, and would they please come back when the sale officially begins. Some Nervy Nancys will accept this answer, but others will leave (or hang up the telephone) in a huff. If

How to handle rude people.

you are a garage sale holder for the first time, the idea of someone leaving your doorstep or hanging up the telephone in such a state might be disquieting. Don't let it be. Remember, the majority of your customers are waiting patiently for your sale to begin.

Nervy Nancys are guilty of other maneuvers calculated to loosen you from your sense of fairness and sanity. Besides wanting to attend your sale before it actually begins, Nervy Nancys will ask you to put items aside so they can think about buying them, or torment, badger, and berate you into selling an item at even more of a bargain price. Do not be misled by their incredible array of excuses and reasons for wanting things done *their* way. Believe me, they are ingenious in their abilities of getting you to reset the policies of your sale.

Remember, most of your customers will be pleasant and friendly. But, you will enjoy your garage sale even more if you are prepared to handle the Nervy Nancys.

4. Collectors: I think collectors are the most difficult customers to deal with, because they usually do know their stuff. However, you do not have to be intimidated by them if you have had your merchandise appraised, know what it is worth, and have priced it reasonably.

5. Dealers: I *love* dealers and I have found dealers to be among my best customers. Why? Because dealers know what they are doing, come prepared with money, and usually buy a great deal of merchandise. In fact, at one of our sales, a dealer literally bought half of our merchandise.

Unfortunately, there are some dealers who are Nervy Nancys. But the majority of them are professionals and extremely business-like.

Sometimes a dealer will ask you for a discount. If the dealer is buying a large number of items, give a discount. It is well deserved.

6. Friends, Neighbors, and Relatives: The most difficult problem you will encounter with friends, neighbors, and relatives is that they usually expect the privilege of picking over your stuff before sale day officially begins. If you think turning down strangers is difficult, just wait until you are challenged with saying "no" to your best friend! But, you must say no because it would not be fair to your other customers to let someone buy things before sale day. Here is a scenario to aid you in meeting the challenge of saying no to friends, neighbors, and relatives:

> *A person reads your classified ad, drools over your description of an antique chair, waits patiently for Saturday to arrive, drives twenty miles to your home, stands outside a shut garage door (with fifty other people), watches the garage door open, enters your showroom, and spies the antique chair with a big "Sold" sign on it.*

Not a very nice scenario, is it?

The way to handle friends, neighbors, and relatives is to let them look at what you've got, if they absolutely must, but to not let them buy anything until sale day. I will always admire one neighbor who had her eye on a brand new football as a Christmas present for her son. She never even asked me if she could buy it before the sale; she simply told me she had her eye on it. On sale day, the first item I sold was that football. And I'm sure you know whom I sold it to.

I hope all your customers will be as considerate as my neighbor. Most will be. But for the ones who aren't, my advice is: practice saying "no" and smiling at the same time.

Sale Day Will Be Filled With Excitement

You will begin to feel a certain amount of excitement before your sale begins, even as early as when you are displaying your merchandise and thinking about receiving money for items you detest and can't wait to sell. Then, on the morning of sale day, as you see people driving up your street and parking station wagons and pick-up trucks in front of your home, your excitement will increase. Finally, when you open your doors and let a stream of people into your sale, your excitement level will be at its peak.

Don't be surprised if you are nervous. It is normal to be nervous, especially for the first-time garage sale holder. Once you begin receiving money for your merchandise, however, the nervousness will dissipate and the enjoyment will take over.

Sale Day Will Be Filled With Surprises

I'm going to mention some of the surprises you will experience on sale day so they won't be quite as sur-

Sale day will be filled with surprises. You'll sell items you never thought would sell.

prising as if I hadn't mentioned them at all, but you will still feel a certain amount of surprise when you experience these phenomena for yourself:

1. Things you thought would never sell, will. Things you thought would sell, might not.
2. You will sell the most merchandise and make the most money during the first few hours of your sale—maybe even during the first thirty minutes of your sale.
3. You will be so emotionally and physically exhausted after your sale, you will probably just want to grab a bite to eat, watch some television, and go to sleep. You may not even have the energy to count all the money you have made.

What Else Will Happen On Sale Day?

After your sale has been in progress for a while, the pace will slow down. This is a good time to change prices, rearrange your merchandise, and pretty things up a bit. Toward the late afternoon, you may get another rush of people. We have sold some of our most expensive items toward the end of the day.

On the second day of your sale, if you have one, you will be amazed at the difference in the number of people who attend. Most of the time, although not always, the second day is quieter than the first. Fewer people will come by, and you may begin to feel a letdown. Don't let it bother you too much; the let-down is normal. After all, you have been planning sale day for weeks, and soon your garage sale will just be a memory. Ah, but a wonderful memory, I hope. Think of all the money you have made and all the merchandise you have sold. Now, that ought to make you feel better. If you have planned, prepared, and advertised your sale wisely, you will probably be extremely pleased with the results of all your efforts.

What To Do With The Merchandise That Doesn't Sell

Even at the end of the most successful sales, there will be leftover unsold merchandise. There are three things you can do with this leftover merchandise.

Store It For Your Next Garage Sale

Keeping in mind that you *never stop receiving unwanted gifts or buying things you never use,* leftover merchandise can be stored in one place and used as the nucleus for your next garage sale. Always remember, if something didn't sell this time around, it might sell at your next sale

Donate The Leftover Merchandise To Charity

This is quite simple to do. Many communities have an emergency aid organization that would be delighted to receive whatever you have left over from your sale. Or, you can give the stuff to Goodwill or to the Salvation Army. Most charities will even come and pick the stuff up. When you donate items to these organizations, you can usually claim the donation as a deduction on your income tax return.

Sell It To A Used Furniture Or Junk Dealer

All you have to do is pick up your telephone, call one of these dealers, and say, "Come on over." Be prepared, however; a used furniture dealer or junk dealer never gives you anything near the value of your merchandise. But think of it this way: If you sell your remaining merchandise to a dealer, you have made even *more* money at your garage sale!

Well, I have told you everything I know about how to hold a very successful garage sale. If you plan, organize, and prepare for your sale according to my instructions, I truly believe you will have a wonderful experience. Garage sales are fun *and* extremely profitable. So, get out those dollar-sign eyeglasses, think *money,* and go to work! I have my fingers crossed, and I hope your garage sale will be an exciting, enjoyable, and lucrative experience for you.

Like sitting ducks, wooden decoy ducks wait to be bought.

PART II

CAREERS FOR GARAGE SALE ENTHUSIASTS

HOUSEHOLD LIQUIDATORS OF ATLANTA

WE ARE QUALIFIED AGENTS TO SELL THE ENTIRE OR PARTIAL
CONTENTS OF YOUR HOME, APARTMENT OR ESTATE. WE ASSUME
ALL COSTS, SUPPLY PERSONNEL AND ASSURE THE GREATEST
RETURN. WE ARE LICENSED AND REGISTERED. ALL DONE IN
A SINGLE WEEKEND WITH DIGNITY AND PROFIT TO YOU. WHAT
AN EASY WAY TO SELL, MOVE, OR REDECORATE. USE OUR OPEN
HOUSE SALE METHOD. WE ORGANIZE, TAG, ADVERTISE, AND
SELL IN AN EASY AND QUICK WAY. NO HOME TOO LARGE OR
TOO SMALL. WE HAVE A TREMENDOUS FOLLOWING. CALL US AT
993-6026 OR 993-1244 FOR AN APPOINTMENT.

JUDY AND BRUCE HIMELFARB

Judy Himelfarb of Household Liquidators of Atlanta says "I hand out flyers to real estate people, decorators, bankers, etc., and whenever I do a sale I keep a stack of flyers by the door."

CHAPTER 6

HOW TO START A
LIQUIDATION BUSINESS

IF YOU HAVE HELD a few garage sales of your own and have enjoyed doing so, have I got a career for you! Why not start your own liquidation business!

Professional liquidators are people who will go to other people's homes, price and display their unwanted possessions, and then sell these undesired treasures at either an auction or a glorified garage sale.

In short, professional liquidators do all the work, while *you* sit back and relax.

"If you don't want to be bothered, or you don't have the time to sell your unwanted belongings, why not let me do it for you?" suggests Judy Himelfarb of Household Liquidators of Atlanta, an Atlanta-based company whose sole purpose is to help other people rid themselves—either because they are moving, redecorating, or trying to unload a voluminous amount of inherited goods—of possessions they no longer want.

Judy and Bruce Himelfarb (Judy handles the day-to-day running of the business) started Household Liquidators of Atlanta several years ago after Judy helped a friend with a moving sale. The friend was duly impressed with Judy's capabilities and told her, "You should do this for a living—you're good!"

Judy went home and told Bruce what her friend had said. Together they agreed that the liquidation business was an excellent part-time job for Judy. (You can make your own hours and handle as many sales as you want.)

According to the Himelfarbs, the ideal attributes a person needs in order to become a successful professional liquidator are: (1) an excellent business sense; (2) the courage to meet the public; (3) a good personality; (4) a basic knowledge of what things are worth (Judy says, "You start off with a basic knowledge, but you learn and learn and learn as you go along. For valuables like collectibles and antiques, though, we still occasionally need to call in an appraiser!"); and (5) a mentor to teach you the business ("We had a friend who really taught us the ropes!" adds Judy).

If you think you would like to start your own liquidation business, the following list of things to do should get you started in the right direction:

1. Prowl through department stores, antique shops, flea markets, and garage sales. This gives you a good idea of not only what things are worth, but also how much other people are willing to pay for them. Attend auctions and

estate sales for the same reasons. You must build up a storehouse of knowledge about prices.

2. Try to find someone who owns a liquidation business in another city. Since you won't be any competition, ask them to share their professional tips with you about how to operate a successful liquidation business. If they agree, listen carefully and take notes.

3. Get to know and cultivate the friendships of appraisers, antique shop owners, real estate agents, bankers, insurance agents, and interior decorators. All of these people are a source of potential clients for you. Tell them you are thinking about going into the liquidation business and would appreciate any clients they can send your way after you officially start your business. And, when you do officially start your business, don't forget to notify them that you have done so.

4. When you feel confident you can do a super job for your first client, obtain a business license (usual fee is $50.00 to $100.00) from the appropriate authority in your community.

5. Hire an accountant to set up your bookkeeping system.

6. Open a business checking account.

7. Have business cards and stationery printed up with your name, address, and telephone number.

8. Launch an advertising campaign to publicize your new business. Word of mouth, flyers, and

This garage sale holder (leaning over the command post) was

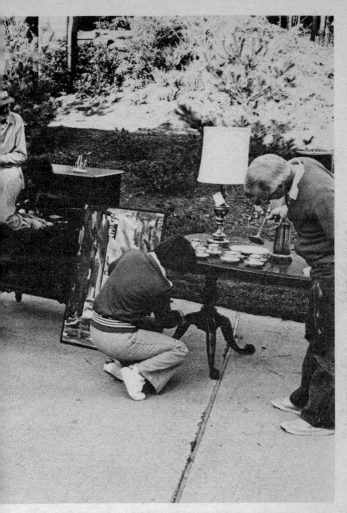

undoubtedly happy with the financial results from her sale.

an advertisement in your local newspaper are good places to start.

9. Announce to the world that you are now a professional liquidator.

10. Wait for the telephone to ring.

"If you do your homework properly," advises Judy, "don't be surprised when you get your first telephone call from a potential client. Of course, you *will* be surprised and excited and nervous. But, don't show it. After all, the caller doesn't know he/she is your first client. Besides, it's the results that count. If you do a super job, they won't care if they were your first or one-thousandth client. The best feeling in the world is when the telephone rings and the caller says, 'Hello. My name is Mrs. So-and-So. You did a marvelous job for my friend. She raved about you. Could you please help me, too?' "

If the caller asks you to help, then the next step is to set up an initial interview at the client's home. The purpose of holding an interview with clients at their homes is threefold: (1) the client and the liquidator meet face to face and hopefully establish a good rapport; (2) the liquidator is able to personally evaluate the amount and estimated value of the merchandise the client wants to sell (this is important because if the client doesn't have enough valuable merchandise, the liquidator must decide then and there whether or not to do the sale. Also, the liquidator must know the kinds of merchandise the client will be selling so that the liquidator, if necessary, can contact the appropriate appraisers); and (3) the liquidator can get a feel for the location of the sale—i.e., does the location have enough space to comfortably accommodate a sale? is the location sheltered? does the location pose any problems as far as blocking off the rest of the home is concerned? etc.

Besides establishing a client/liquidator rapport, evaluating the merchandise, and checking out the location of the sale, the following other matters are discussed during the initial interview with the client:

The Fee For The Liquidator's Services

Liquidators either charge a flat fee or a percentage (15 to 25 per cent) of the gross proceeds from the sale as payment for their services.

Many liquidators have standard flat fees, which guarantee that they will make a profit from each sale they conduct. They know what their basic overhead is, what they believe their services are worth, and have arrived at a flat fee figure which ensures the payment of both. They will not conduct a sale for a client unless the gross proceeds from the sale of the merchandise will be greater than their standard flat fee.

I know you would like for me to state a range of prices for flat fees, but I can't. Flat fees are determined by where you live (city, suburbs, country), how much the going rate is to place classified advertisements and to hire people to help you run a sale, and what kind of reputation you have for being a successful liquidator. Obviously, someone who has been conducting liquidation sales for ten years is going to demand (and get) a bigger flat fee (and thus, a bigger profit from conducting sales) than someone who is starting out in the profession. However, just because you are a neophyte liquidator doesn't mean you shouldn't make a profit from running a sale for a client. So, be smart. Estimate the value of each potential client's merchandise, what you expect your overhead to be, and whether or not you can make a profit from conducting that particular sale *before* you agree to run it.

The same considerations should apply if you decide to charge a percentage of the gross proceeds as payment for your services.

The Responsibilities of the Liquidators

Pricing, displaying and selling merchandise; preparing for, paying for, and executing an advertising campaign; and hiring and paying for any additional help needed at the sale—i.e., sales/security personnel, "strong men," and cleaning people.

What The Policy Will Be Regarding Whether Or Not The Client Will Be Present During The Sale.

The Himelfarbs prefer the client not to be present during the sale because many clients become nostalgic after the sale has begun and, thus, find it difficult to part with certain items after previously deciding to sell them. Also, some clients interfere with the proceedings by joining in during the wheeling and dealing of selling.

The Merchandise That Isn't Sold

The following means of disposing of this merchandise are discussed with the client: (1) giving it to charity and taking the donation as a tax deduction on their income tax return, and (2) selling it to a used furniture dealer for a small price, with emphasis on the "small."

The Contract

Finally, if the client and the liquidator agree on all the above matters, either a handshake or a written contract firms up the deal. The Himelfarbs, for instance, do not use a written contract.

After the initial interview is conducted, the liquidator goes to work. Here, generously provided by the Himelfarbs, is a chronological list of activities the liquidator engages in to prepare for and organize a liquidation sale:

STEP NUMBER ONE—Get To Know Your Merchandise: Go back to the client's home and go through the merchandise carefully. Sometimes a client has boxes and cartons filled with possessions. Open up each box and each carton, and check out their contents. Count the number of place-settings of silver or china. Count the number of glassware. Really get to know your client's merchandise as if it were your own.

STEP NUMBER TWO—Design And Launch An Advertising Campaign: The usual advertising campaign consists of one or more of the following: flyers, word of mouth, signs (when permitted by law), classified ads (appealing to dealers and interior decorators), and, if the client is extremely wealthy or a celebrity, mailed invitations to the sale.

The liquidator pays for the entire advertising campaign.

STEP NUMBER THREE—Contact Professional Appraisers (When Needed): The liquidators may decide to contact professional appraisers to appraise certain items the client wants to sell. Appraisers get paid for their services either by receiving first pick of anything to be sold (this usually occurs if the appraiser is also a dealer), or by a fee determined by a percentage of the value of whatever is appraised.

The liquidator must pay for the appraiser if the appraiser doesn't want first pick.

STEP NUMBER FOUR—Hire Additional Help For Sale (When Needed): There are three types of additional help a liquidator may need to help with a liquidation sale:

1. Sales/Security People

Whether or not a liquidator will need additional sales/security people at a liquidation sale depends on the size of the sale area (if the sale is a moving sale or an estate sale, the sale will take place throughout the entire house, thus, stationing a sales/security person in each room of the house is a wise idea), and the value of the items being sold (obviously, if valuable merchandise is going to be sold, you will need to have additional people watching the sale area).

2. "Strong Men"

If there is a lot of heavy furniture to move around, it pays to have at least one, and preferably two, "strong men" to do it.

3. Cleaning People

If there is a great deal of merchandise to sell, cleaning people are *not* a luxury; they are a necessity.

Hire additional sales help.

The liquidator pays for any additional help hired for the sale.

STEP NUMBER FIVE—Price, Inventory, And Display Merchandise: The liquidator puts a price tag on each item. At the customer's request, the liquidator will list all items to be sold on a master inventory list before putting them on display tables.

STEP NUMBER SIX—Sale Day: The liquidator arrives at least one hour before the sale is to begin, gives instructions to the people who will be helping at the sale, closes off the rest of the home, if necessary, checks to make certain everything is ready to begin, and sets up a cashier's command post by the exit. It is wise to have both an entrance and an exit for the sale so that traffic can flow easily. The liquidator should also station someone at the entrance of the sale to welcome people and answer any questions.

If the area of the sale isn't spacious, or if the client is extremely wealthy or a celebrity, it is a good idea to allow only a small number of people into the sale area at any one time. This is not only for security reasons, but for cutting down on the number of curiosity-seekers as well.

If there will be large pieces of merchandise sold, it is very important to have large signs saying that the liquidator is not responsible for removing these big pieces from the sale area. "Customers must make their own arrangements for moving these items. Some items need special care when being moved, like pianos. It takes five men to properly move a grand piano. I always explain the special instructions needed to move an item when it is sold. I also explain to the buyer that I would appreciate their payment for the item, before they move it," says Judy.

After the sale is over, the liquidator adds up the proceeds of the sale, writes a check—minus her fee—to the client, pays her additional help, takes down whatever signs are displayed, removes all of her paraphernalia, telephones a used furniture dealer to remove the remaining merchandise (if customer wants to dispose of the leftover merchandise in this manner), and leaves. The liquidator's job is over. It is the responsibility of the client to put their home back in order and dispose of the remaining merchandise either by consulting with the used furniture dealer or by donating it to charity.

The Himelfarbs agree that the professional liquidation business is an enjoyable and profitable career for a husband and wife to share. But you don't have to be a husband and wife team. You can be two good friends who want to go into business together. Or, you could go into business by yourself. In any event, I hope this chapter on how to start your own liquidation business has inspired you to think about branching out from having semi-annual garage sales to having weekly sales for other people.

"Doesn't Phyllis have the best junk?"

• CHAPTER 7 •

HOW TO BECOME A FLEA MARKET DEALER

I ASKED REED SAVAGE, a friend who is a successful flea market dealer, how to start a flea market business and he answered, "One begins a flea market business by simply knowing one's talents. If one of these talents expresses itself in this type of atmosphere," he flung open his arms to symbolically embrace the hundreds of people strolling along the booth-bordered aisles of the Atlanta Flea Market, "then all one needs to do is obtain a business license, pack some things from home (either homemade crafts or unwanted possessions), rent a booth from a flea market owner, and you're in business."

"Come on, Reed," I prodded, "isn't that over-simplifying it a bit?"

"Not really," he answered.

With apologies to Reed, I didn't believe him. I said to myself, "I can't believe it is *that* easy to start a flea market business," and I set out wandering down the maze of aisles in order to query other flea market dealers about the intricacies of breaking into the business.

I needn't have bothered. Reed was right. Without exception, every flea market dealer gave me the same advice about how to start a flea market business. Apparently, it is incredibly easy to become a flea market dealer. According to every dealer I spoke with, all you need to do is obtain a business license, decide what you want to sell (and procure sufficient quantities of it to be able to sell enough merchandise to pay for the overhead of your first flea market outing), rent a booth from the owner of a flea market, and presto—you're in the flea market business.

The easiest part of owning and operating a flea market business is starting it up; the hard part is keeping it going. But, if you can make a profit doing it, what a pleasant way to make a second income or a full-time living. For starters, you are your own boss. You run the show. You set your own business hours and have the luxury of knowing that no one will complain if you show up ten minutes late for work. But perhaps the most enticing reason for going into the flea market business is the fact that your initial capital investment is so small (a business license costs between $50.00 and $100.00, and renting a booth for the day can cost as little as $5.00). Also, if you don't want to invest in the start-up costs of assembling an inventory of stock, bring a bunch of stuff from home. No wonder there are so many people going into the flea market business!

I know it sounds fantastic, but before you start

loading up your car with cartons of unwanted possessions, remember that the easy part of operating a flea market business is starting it up and the hard part is keeping it going successfully. So, to help you get started in the right direction, and to keep you going, here is a basic primer on the flea market business.

The Flea Market Primer

The Different Kinds Of Flea Markets

There are many different kinds of flea markets. There are outdoor flea markets and indoor ones, flea markets that operate one weekend a month and others that are open every weekend of each month. A flea market that is open each weekend of the month is called a permanent flea market, and most of the dealers I spoke to believe that a beginner should rent space at a permanent flea market when starting out in the business, rather than tackling the traveling flea market circuit.

From what the experienced dealers tell me, the traveling flea market circuit can be a rough life for the neophyte. Until one can get used to the routine of unpacking merchandise, packing merchandise, traveling, unpacking merchandise, etc., he or she usually suffers from chronic fatigue. One must condition oneself to the job of working *and* traveling at the same time, which is that much harder to do if you are learning the business simultaneously.

If you have a choice of permanent flea markets near your home, pick the one that has the best reputation (from a dealer's point of view) and the most customers. Both of these considerations are easy to check out—go to each flea market and ask the dealers if they are happy with the management, with the security the management provides, with the number of customers who attend the flea market, etc. By carefully listening to their answers, you will get an excellent idea of which flea market you want to rent space at.

Merchandise

If you have ever been to a flea market, you know that you can sell anything and everything at one. I have seen a dealer specializing in the sale of green parrots, another dealer whose only merchandise consisted of rows of beer cans, and a woman who sold turn-of-the-century children's toys. You may decide to specialize in a certain type of merchandise from the moment you decide to go into the flea market business. Or, you may decide to simply bring a bunch of your unwanted items from home. The only rule is *have enough merchandise.* Reed told me of several unfortunate cases in which flea market rookies were forced to go out of business because even if they had sold everything displayed in their booths (not much), they still would not have made enough money to pay their overhead.

Speaking of having enough merchandise to sell, eventually you will have to restock your inventory. If you become a successful flea market dealer, you will soon find that you will be spending your "off" days (Monday through Thursday) trying to locate more merchandise to sell. Finding more merchandise to sell, an activity frantically engaged in by every flea

Rich Lang, one of our photographers, got so carried away at this yard sale that he bought a camera case and two brass cylinders.

Why the brass cylinders? He said he's going to make them into lamps and give them away as Christmas gifts.

market dealer to whom I spoke, is simultaneously fun, time-consuming, exhilarating, frustrating, pleasurable, a nuisance, and absolutely necessary if you want to continue making money as a flea market dealer. Many times the search for more merchandise means traveling to other flea markets in order to find good merchandise at decent prices. Many times, though, a dealer simply picks up the telephone and answers newspaper "For Sale" ads. Reed said that "replenishing your supply of merchandise is probably the most challenging and exciting aspect of owning a flea market business."

When it comes time for you to replenish *your* supply of merchandise, here are some sources you can use:

1. Other flea market dealers
2. Garage sales, carport sales, moving sales, etc.
3. Estate sales
4. Bankruptcy sales
5. Antique shops
6. Manufacturers' sales
7. Newspaper "For Sale" ads
8. Placing your own ads in newspapers (For example, "We buy anything—ANYTHING! Call: [404] 999-9999")

Pricing Your Merchandise

Crafts: If your particular craft is a common one, such as candlemaking or jewelry designing, the best way to learn how to price your creative endeavors is to stroll through a flea market and note what other candlemakers and jewelry designers are getting for their merchandise.

If, however, your craft is rather unusual—for example, you make furniture out of rolled-up newspapers—you will have to resort to trial and error pricing. Trial and error pricing means that if your dream is to turn your rolled-up newspaper furniture hobby into a business and you rent a flea market booth for the weekend to make this dream a reality, and you don't sell any of your furniture during the entire weekend, either your prices were too high or, worse, your rolled-up newspaper furniture is wretchedly unattractive. On the other hand, if you sold out your entire stock in less than two hours, you may have been giving it away and never knew it.

Each craft will have its unique pricing problems, but a good rule of thumb is: for every item sold, a third of the price should go toward overhead (cost of materials, booth rental, travel expenses, etc.); another third should go toward your time, energy, and sweat in making the item; and the last third should go toward profit—*your* profit. Because many crafts people say that their "profit" frequently gets lost in the hustle and bustle of trying to keep their craft businesses afloat, it would be wise for you to not quit your uninteresting, full-time, money-in-the-bank, nine-to-five job until you are positive that you can turn your hobby into a profitable venture.

Used Furniture, Clothing, Appliances: The rule of thumb is to price these items at a 100 percent markup of the price you paid. Present market value is what counts when pricing merchandise that falls into this category. If you bought an old Motorola record player for $5.00 and its present market value (according to the price other dealers are setting for old Motorola record players) is $7.00, you paid too much for it because you will probably not be able to sell it for a 100 percent markup ($10.00). You must be extremely careful when you buy merchandise for resale. You must be the one to get the *real* bargain so that you can pass on a medium bargain to your customers.

Antiques and Collectibles: Pricing antiques and collectibles should be classified as an art form. It takes talent and skill to consistently come up with the best prices for this category of merchandise. By "best prices" I mean a price which means you neither give an item away (by putting too low a price on it) nor retain it for posterity (by putting too high a price on it). Most flea market dealers have their own personal formulas for arriving at their prices, but when I pressed them for details, the majority admitted that their formulas were really a combination of factors: knowing the present market value of an item (obtained by looking in a recent pricing guide like *Kovel's*, which is available in most bookstores); taking into consideration what the dealer paid for the item when he bought it; and intuition about the price someone else will pay for the item.

Some dealers have the skill to price items well, even from the moment they open their businesses, and other dealers must learn the skill. But, if you spend time studying the prices other dealers are getting for similar merchandise, if you study the recent pricing guides, and cultivate the friendships of other dealers who will be willing to teach you some of their expertise, you certainly will be way ahead in the flea market pricing arena.

Bookkeeping

There are two types of record-keeping systems you should initiate when you decide you want to go into the flea market business. The first type of record-keeping system is to keep track of your inventory. The second type of record-keeping is to keep track of your financial situation. You should start both systems before you sell your first piece of merchandise.

Your Inventory Record-Keeping System: It is good business sense to keep track of what you buy and sell. Keeping an up-to-date record takes time, but it is easy to do and worth the time spent doing it. The easiest method to use for inventory control is to buy a lined notebook. On the first page, rule off nine columns. The headings of the columns should be: Inventory Number; Date; My Check Number; Amount; Item; Where Purchased; Where Sold; Date; and Amount Sold For. Each time you buy an item, assign it an inventory number and fill out the appropriate information in each column. Then, on a price tag, write the inventory number you have given the item and the item's price. When you sell the item, jot down its inventory number and the price you sold the item for. Then, to complete your inventory record, complete the remaining blank columns in your notebook with the information you now have about when you sold the item and to whom you sold it.

By keeping an up-to-date inventory of your merchandise, you will begin to learn what sells and what doesn't sell, whether or not your prices are reasonable (or whether the original price you wrote down for an item consistently varies from the price it actually sold for), and you will have a record, for insurance purposes, of what you owned if a loss occurs due to theft, fire, etc.

Your Financial Record-Keeping System: I don't have to remind you that the Internal Revenue Service is always interested in your financial situation. When no one else cares whether or not you are making it or blowing it, the IRS will care, and they will especially care if you are making it *big*.

So to appease the IRS and to aid you in making payments to the sales tax unit of your state (most states will expect you to obtain a sales tax number if you are regularly doing business), it is extremely wise for you to keep a record of your accounts receivable (the money you make selling merchandise) and your accounts payable (the money you pay out for expenses).

For the neophyte flea market dealer, you do not need to start out with a sophisticated set of books. Again, a lined notebook will do. Divide the notebook into two sections. Label the first section Accounts Receivable and the second section Accounts Payable.

On the first page of your accounts receivable section, rule off four columns and assign them the following headings: Date; To Whom; Description; and Amount. As you sell items, list them by date in your accounts receivable section. At the end of each month, add up the money you made. Then, either skip a few lines and start a new month or go on to the next page and rule off four more columns.

Your accounts payable section should have a minimum of five columns with the following headings: Date; My Check No.; To Whom; For What;

and Amount Paid. Every time you pay a bill, every time you pay for gas to travel to and from a flea market, every time you buy something to use for displaying merchandise, and every time you buy more merchandise, list the expense by date in your accounts payable section. At the end of the month, add up these expenses.

You can quickly find out if you have made a profit during the first month of your business. Simply subtract the amount you paid out for expenses from the amount you received in payment for merchandise. If you made a profit—fantastic!

If you show a steadily increasing profit each month, after several months you may decide to hire an accountant to set up a more sophisticated set of books for you. But, until that time, this easy bookkeeping system should provide you with enough information to calculate your sales tax and (ugh!), pay your other taxes.

Your First Day As A Flea Market Dealer

Well, the big day has finally arrived. Your merchandise is packed in cartons, and the cartons are packed in the trunk of your car. You are nervous and excited and happy. You should be. New doors are going to open for you because, as of today, you are a flea market dealer. Here are some suggestions for making your first day as enjoyable as it can possible be:

1. **Arrive Early:** Do this for two reasons: (1) You have never set up a booth before and until you have done it a few times, this soon-to-be routine task will take

longer for you than for the other flea market dealers. Also, the other flea market dealers will probably be interested in getting to know you and your merchandise. To prevent becoming flustered with all their attention, get to the flea market early and set up your booth. Then, you will be able to relax and enjoy their comradeship. (2) Early birds get the best spots to set up—unless it is a permanent flea market where dealers have reserved spaces.

2. Make Your Display Tables Look As Attractive As Possible: For hints on how to do this, see Chapter 3.

3. Bring The Following Items With You:

Folding tables (if the management doesn't provide them)

Coverings for your display tables

A folding chair or stool

Plenty of change (dollar bills and coins)

Shopping bags and newspapers to wrap merchandise in

Receipt books, sales books, price tags, pens and pencils, poster board for making signs, and lunch

If the flea market is outdoors, bring rain equipment plus plastic see-through coverings for your display tables.

4. Wear An Article Of Clothing That Has Pockets: (so you can keep your money on your person)

5. If At All Possible, Bring A Friend: A friend isn't just companionship. A friend means you can take breaks when you need to go to the restroom facilities. A friend will help you carry things to your booth and then back to your car. And, a friend will bolster your spirits if business isn't good.

I asked Reed what his secret was for operating a successful flea market business, and he said, "Be reasonable, logical, industrious, responsible, thoughtful, and practical." If you do all these things, you are bound to be successful in your new flea market business.

DATE DUE